This book belongs to:

____

Made in the USA
Las Vegas, NV
19 August 2021

28422660R10066